ASK TO LISTEN

Discerning the Voice of God

SOULSHIFT
Bible Study

Dave Ward

wesleyan
publishing
house

Indianapolis, Indiana

Copyright © 2012 by College Wesleyan Church of Marion, Indiana
Published by Wesleyan Publishing House
Indianapolis, Indiana 46250
Printed in the United States of America
ISBN: 978-0-89827-481-3

Writer: Dave Ward

Some names have been changed to protect the privacy of individuals.

This Bible study is a companion book to Steve DeNeff and David Drury's *SoulShift:
The Measure of a Life Transformed* (Indianapolis, Ind.: Wesleyan Publishing House,
2011).

CONTENTS

INTRODUCTION

Have you heard the fable of the Native American who traveled to New York City? Standing at an intersection, waiting to cross, he caught the eye of a busy New Yorker who was apparently late for an appointment. Feeling the eyes of the Native American on him, the New Yorker muttered, "What are you looking at?"

The Native American only smiled and said, "Can you hear that cricket?"

"Are you kidding?" the New Yorker blurted. "How can you hear a cricket through all of this noise?"

Then the Native American lifted a quarter from his pocket, dropped it onto the sidewalk, and at the sound of the metal clanging on the pavement a half dozen people began searching.

"See that?" said the Native American. "One hears what one listens for!"

Listening is a learned behavior. And listening for God is a fine art. Almost no one does it naturally. Even those who are, by nature, contemplative will only hear their own voice until they learn to listen for God's. And how do we learn? It begins by admitting that, as easy as it sounds, we really *don't* know how to do it. It takes time and practice. It takes discipline and restraint. Then it takes watching someone else do it.

So in this study, I recommend to you our friend, Dave Ward. "Listening is hard work," he once told me. He should know. He's been at it for a few years. The psalmist said, "The LORD confides in those who fear him" (25:14). I wasn't surprised to see things here that others haven't said because . . . well, Dave has learned to listen and, quite frankly, I think God has told him things that he doesn't say to everyone who only asks. I also like Dave's chances of saying this in a language that *everyone* can hear, especially those who grew up in the noise of modern technology.

Like other writers for this series, Dave and his family are members of College Wesleyan Church where he is best known for his preaching. But what makes any preacher great, and what makes Dave so, is his content. He is direct and simple. His advice is uncompromising, but practical. I can't wait for you to dive into this study and to talk about it. But mostly, I hope you will read and listen. As you do, my prayer is that you will become comfortable with silence, that you will be quick to hear what you have listened for, and that you may follow God's voice with boldness.

Steve DeNeff
Senior Pastor, College Wesleyan Church

HOW THIS STUDY WORKS

This four-week *SoulShift* study has two components. You'll do part of it alone and part of it together with a group of people in an existing small group, Bible study, or class. Each week includes five daily readings. You will want to encounter these with a Bible and pen in hand. Each reading has a Scripture reference so you can consider some aspect of moving from Ask to Listen in the context of Scripture. Within the readings, you'll find questions to ponder. You might highlight them and take a moment to think about them right away. Or you can meditate on a question throughout the day.

There are also questions each week for your group to discuss together. Your discussion group may be new or have years of connection. Whatever it is like, use this *SoulShift* study to take things to the next level. Start by sharing from your heart on the issues raised, and how you are being led to shift from Ask to Listen.

Our first instinct in our spiritual lives is to ask. First, we ask our advisors, our friends. We "ask" by reading books or listening to talk radio. We seek the advice of others because we want to learn. This is not bad; it's just where we all start. Over time, we mature to the point where we begin directing these questions to God himself. We begin by asking him for guidance, for a sign, for answers. But we are frustrated that he often does not answer. Or, we discover, he's answering, but he's just answering different questions than we're asking.

Then we learn to hear. We learn to listen in our prayers. We find that God longs to speak, but we are speaking over him. It's not only the noise of this life that drowns out his voice (although it is in part that). It's also our own voices that drown out his. In this study, you'll find a practical and convictional approach in learning to listen to God. Listen to the words of this study first—but all along and from now on listen to God most of all.

WEEK 1

IS LISTENING TO GOD EVEN POSSIBLE?

"How do we discern God's voice? . . . When God speaks,
it is always consistent with his Word and nature.
He doesn't tell you to do things that are
contrary to his Word."[1]

You listen for God's voice? Wacko. Nut case. Those are the names that might come to people's minds when you start saying things like, "God told me." Take heart. Most likely you will not hear God's audible voice in your lifetime.

Why, then, does Scripture say, "My sheep know my voice"?

God's voice is a metaphor. Was Jesus talking about real sheep? Was he speaking of bleating animals? No, Jesus was using sheep as a metaphor for people. Does God have cosmic-size ears that are blown up versions of human ears? Of course not. God certainly *can* speak (Deut. 4:12; 1 Sam. 3:10; Ps. 29). Whatever we "hear" from God, we receive from the Holy Spirit. The Spirit only has a voice that sounds like a human voice when the Spirit wants to have a voice. What I mean by the metaphor of "God's voice" is simply this: God gets through to us.

> "My sheep listen to my voice; I know them, and they follow me."
>
> —John 10:27

If God chooses to get through in the form of a human-like voice, so be it. If God "speaks" in an inner conviction, a bodily sensation, an intuition, words in the mind, an image, a scriptural passage, a hymn, a dream, or a conversation with a spiritual guide, so be it. God "speaks" in any way God wants. God has used rainbows, donkeys, large fish, worms, ants, thunderstorms, and earthquakes to get through to people before. (If you think these are made up, see Gen. 9:12–17; Num. 22:21–34; Jon. 1:17; 4:7; Prov. 6:6–11; 1 Kings 18:45; and Matt. 27:51–53.)

The promise is this: God will communicate with us. That is if we let the Spirit speak to us. This is what it means to listen for God—to let him through and say what he will to us.

There are three parts to this journey of letting God through: trusting, paying attention, and discerning. First, trust that God is trying to get through. Second, pay attention for the innumerable ways and times God may be seeking to get through to you. Third, learn to discern when it is God getting through.

What does this mean practically? Don't crowd out God with busyness, noise, and distraction. Don't drown out God with your fears, insecurities, and opinions. Don't rule out God with your pride, stubbornness, or independence. Trust God to get through. Look for God to get through. Let God get through, especially when it hurts. That is what listening means.

YOUR SOULSHIFT

Go back and read each of these verses two times: John 10:27; Psalm 37:7, 23–24. What does God bring to mind as you read these verses? Can you listen through the verses to hear what God may be trying to communicate to you? Write down any thoughts that come to mind.

When you think about listening for God, what do you fear most?

Take those fears one at a time to God in prayer. Tell God what you are afraid of and quiet yourself. Do any thoughts or responses come to mind? Write them down.

JOHN 8:31–47; MATTHEW 3:17; PROVERBS 1:23

Eve was sleeping on a couch in the lounge where our small group usually met. We invited her to join our group. "Have any of you ever heard God's voice?" Eve asked us one day. I secretly thought she was crazy. I didn't think someone like me could hear from

> "He who belongs to God hears what God says."
> —John 8:47

God. "No? None of you!" Eve looked baffled, "Why not?"

Then Eve began to tell her story. Either she was a talented liar or she had experienced the guidance of God in miraculous ways. Eve came back to our small group three weeks in a row. Because of her stories, I knew I had to try to hear God. I would listen and do whatever I thought God's Spirit led me to do. I would trust whatever I thought came from God. What did I have to lose? Later, I could check to see whether what I thought I heard was confirmed or not. Most of what I thought I heard was disconfirmed. They were products of my own anxiety, imagination, or ambition. After some time, however, I began to recognize the ways God speaks to me.

The first way is through conviction. True conviction does not come nearly as often as my own guilt-trips. I learned the difference slowly. Yet when that conviction was real, if I suppressed it, no other communication came. When I confessed and repented, a flood of other communication seemed to come.

The most frequent way was God's regular communication of his love. And that's not such an easy thing to receive—not when it comes the way it does from God. The Father is abounding in love, lavishes love, sings over us with love, and fills our hearts with love until they brim over . . . if we let him do it.

Those two poles of listening—conviction and love—are the best place for most Christians to begin shifting toward the listening life. When we listen, God most often speaks the word of love and grace. When necessary, the word of conviction comes through clearly. Without these two forms of the same word, we cannot hear what we need to do in the right way.

YOUR SOULSHIFT

Take a few minutes to calm yourself and ask the Holy Spirit to reveal any sins you need to confess. Commit to yourself ahead of time that if something comes to mind, you will confess it to God; then do so. Share these sins with a brother or sister in Christ who is safe to confide in.

Once you have cleared your conscience, listen for the loving words of God. No audible voice may come, but thoughts will. Ask what God thinks of you. If you have confessed and repented and the words that come to mind are of love, then trust them. Hold them. Savor them. If images of love come, embrace them and place them on the shelf of your mind. Treasure them. You need God's words of loving affirmation to live the joyful Christian life.

Why do you think we need to learn to hear love and conviction before we can discern what God would have us do?

DAY

3

PSALM 85:1-8; JEREMIAH 33:1-3;
JOHN 16:7-15

Early in my Christian walk, I often doubted whether God would want to talk. I was confused at why the God who formed mountains, shaped the seas, and crushed nations would want to reveal his thoughts to me (Amos 4:13). I still think a certain level of humility is required. Job, after all, was rebuked for wanting answers to his questions. If anyone deserved an answer, it was Job. But who has given orders to the morning or assigned a place for the dawn (Job 38:12)? Only God.

We need to find a way to avoid the two extremes of demanding prayers and shame-based self-doubt. The Father delights in communicating with his children, both in songs of delight (Zeph. 3:17) and words of correction (Prov. 3:11–12). The Son has been given to us as God's Word in the last days (Heb. 1:1–2). The Spirit fills us to lead us into all truth (John 16:13). God wants to get through to us. God has broken through to us. God will get through to us again.

> "I listen carefully to what God the LORD is saying, for he speaks peace to his faithful people."
>
> —Psalm 85:8 NLT

Perhaps you think that you are not worthy of the communication of God. Isaiah felt the same way (Isa. 6). We do not have to become holy before God will speak to us. God speaks to us so that he can make us holy. God comes first; we come second.

Perhaps you think that God only communicates to special people in special times of transition and change. Yet God always communicates through the written Word. In and through these words of Scripture, the Spirit continues to speak to all ages, times, and situations. Believe that God wants you to learn to hear the Spirit speaking through the Scriptures. Scripture is God-breathed and useful for the Spirit to get through to us (2 Tim. 3:16).

God wants to speak to you, perhaps in thoughts, dreams, or visions. And God wants to get through to you using other Christians, the practices of the Christian faith, and Scripture. The Lord of the universe *does* want to talk. Will you listen?

YOUR SOULSHIFT

What tempts you to think God may not want to speak with you? Take a moment and ask the Spirit to speak to those sources of doubt.

Ask yourself this question throughout today: "If I knew for sure God wanted to speak to me today, how would I change my day?"

DAY

4

PSALM 84; ISAIAH 56:1-8

On a day-long prayer retreat, I sensed God was asking me to go back to school. I did not know why; I just knew it was God's leading. So far in my life, God has always directed me by giving me one place to go. The Spirit does not work that way with everyone. Remembering this peculiar pattern, I asked God if there was a specific school where I should go for my next degree. Immediately, without hesitation, the place came to mind. I didn't put it there and had never thought about it. It just popped into my mind and kept returning. Deep, gut-wrenching fear followed. "I can't get in!" I cried out. "I am not good enough." This degree and school felt way over my head.

"Call to me and I will answer you and tell you great and unsearchable things you do not know."

—Jeremiah 33:3

It was true. I couldn't get in. In faith, though, I looked up the school on the Internet. I printed out biographies of professors. I read the catalogue. I scheduled a visit. Each professor I met said the same thing: "Have you considered applying anywhere else?" It was not very subtle. I knew by the end of my visit that they did not want me as a student. More fear.

I brought my fears to God. One phrase came to mind in response, "You don't have enough time in the day." Was that God or my own fear? I could not shake the phrase, and I knew it rang true. I did not have enough time in the day to study for the tests I would need to take to apply for the degree. I told God if that thought was from him, it was poor consolation.

However, something changed the next day. That night I set the alarm for 7 a.m. and went to bed near midnight as normal. I had never been a morning person. Again I heard God's diagnosis of "not enough time in the day."

I woke up at 5 a.m. Not normal. The next day I woke up just before 5 a.m., feeling rested and ready to get to work. It has been six years since that day. I have never needed an alarm clock since.

YOUR SOULSHIFT

Take a few moments and journal about how both thoughts are true for you: "There is not enough time in the day," and "My heart and flesh cry out for the living God" (Ps. 84:2).

Circle the three activities you would prefer to do and pray about the result:

- Spend an hour in listening prayer
- Spend an hour doing your favorite hobby
- Spend an hour listening for God in Scripture
- Spend an hour watching your favorite TV show
- Spend an hour journaling what you have learned from God
- Spend an hour surfing your favorite spots on the Internet

Ask God to show you when you might have ten minutes today to listen in silence and pray. Write that time down, and give it to God today.

DAY 5

PSALM 63; PROVERBS 6:6-10; 26:14; MARK 1:32-38

In the last reading, I told you how God started waking me up. Have you ever considered letting God wake you up? Maybe waking up isn't your job; maybe getting up is. Proverbs tells us that the sluggard turns in bed like a door turns on its hinges (Prov. 26:14). Can you picture it? A person wakes up, but turns over to one side to get more sleep. They wake anew and immediately swing back again.

> "Awake, my soul!
> Awake, harp and lyre!
> I will awaken the dawn."
> —Psalm 57:8

Asking does not take much time at all. "Lord, please keep my children safe." Two seconds. "God please remove this sin from me." Three seconds if you say it with deep feeling. "God please give Sally healing from her cancer. In Jesus' name I pray. Amen." Five seconds.

On the other hand, listening takes a lot of time. You probably do not have enough time in the day to do it well. Unless you let God wake you up.

I mean this in two very different ways. First, listen for when God thinks you should usually be going to bed. Write down the time that comes to mind: _____. Go to bed at that time. Consider it a matter of obedience. Before you go to bed, make God this promise: If you wake me up, I will get up. Then simply make listening the first thing you do.

God may put the thought in your mind, "This is your time to get that project done. Have fun." God may just show you a sunrise and warm up your smile. God may say, "Nine at night is a better time for you to be with me." Listen and trust. This does not mean you will become a morning person. I certainly still am not. But since I am up earlier than most people, I seem like it by the time they see me.

Second, let God wake you up after you are already awake. We sleep through half our waking days. Learn to be aware of the opportunities you have through the day to listen. Pay attention to your spare time and small reminders of God's presence. Each of these are God's attempt to wake you up in the middle of the day.

YOUR SOULSHIFT

What are the biggest obstacles to setting a regular bed time? Which of these is in your control?

What intentional actions could you take to make listening early in your day more attractive?

Psalm 63 indicates that sometimes God's wakeup call is in the "watches of the night" (v. 6). Pay attention in the next week and see when God seems to wake you up. Is it at night or in the morning? Listen to God in those moments. Write in a journal if it helps focus your thoughts.

GROUP DISCUSSION GUIDE

If this is your first meeting as a group, you will want to set the tone from the start. Prepare by reading, reflecting, and praying. This week's discussion focuses on the possibility of listening to God. The readings cover concerns such as whether or not God wants to communicate with us, how he communicates with us, our own potential to ignore him, and our lack of time and energy to listen. If you have nagging concerns about whether it is even possible to hear from God, this is the time to talk about them in your group.

LEADER TIPS

Allow some time at the beginning of the meeting either to get to know each other's names and lives or to get reacquainted. Open the more focused time of your meeting with a word of prayer. Listen for the obstacles your group recognizes in their lives to receiving this SoulShift. Write them down for further prayer and discussion later on.

QUESTIONS

In your readings this week, was there a Scripture verse that seemed to connect with you more meaningfully than others? If so, share with the group what you think God is saying to you through it.

The readings made clear that the voice of God is not necessarily audible. How has God found a way to get through to you in the past?

As you read this week, fears and questions probably came up regarding listening to God. Share one or two of those with the group. Take a moment to stop and pray in the group over each of these out loud. Then take two minutes to listen in silence. Share what comes to mind.

The readings spoke of two different kinds of awakenings God can give: physical awakening at night or in the morning and mental awakening through the day. Share one of your experiences in letting God wake you up this week.

Conclude your time as a group by sharing your hopes for the next few weeks of your group meetings. What do you hope will happen for you? Have one person close in prayer asking God to answer these prayers of the heart.

WEEK 2

THE LISTENING CYCLE

"In this shift, you listen with your heart for the still, small voice of God instead of looking for it in the fire, thunder, or wind. It is in this still, small voice that you find simplicity; you discover he is speaking to you and you trust your ability to know it."[2]

DAY
1

JAMES 5:13-19; 1 KINGS 17

Elijah was a person just like us. Think about that for one minute, and you realize that Elijah was absolutely *not* a person just like us. He raised people from the dead, turned dwindling oil into an endless supply, was fed by ravens in a famine, and was taken up to heaven in a flaming chariot. Elijah did not live a life just like anyone you and I have ever known.

I think that is James' point. Elijah's life was different. Yet Elijah was fundamentally, absolutely, and completely the same in his composition. He was thoroughly human. Go back and read 1 Kings 18–20. Notice all the signs of Elijah's humanness. He was afraid, ran from danger, fell unconscious from exhaustion, and felt lonely and weak. He became depressed. Does that sound familiar? That's you. That's me. Elijah was a person just like us, *but* . . .

That word says a lot. James pointed to the contrast. He was just like us, but he lived so incredibly differently. He was just like us, but he knew God so much more intimately. James wanted his readers to see the key difference between our common humanity and the different degrees of closeness to God we experience, both in relationship and results. Elijah was a person just like us, but "he prayed earnestly" (James 5:17).

There's the key: Elijah's prayer life was the difference. We need to ask how Elijah prayed if we want to know how to transcend our humanity and participate in God's glory. Today, focus on one aspect of his prayer life from 1 Kings. Elijah prayed some stupid prayers.

"Elijah was a man just like us. He prayed earnestly."
—James 5:17

I know I shouldn't use the word *stupid*, but I haven't been able to find a better word to describe the things for which Elijah prayed. "He prayed earnestly that it would not rain, and it did not rain on the land for three and a half years" (James 5:17). Now that is a dumb prayer. When it doesn't rain, crops fail, animals die, and humans starve. Elijah prayed for the very thing that could possibly kill everyone he knew and loved, including himself. Only suicidal sociopaths would pray this way.

That is, of course, unless they listened first. This is the key characteristic of Elijah's prayer life. He did not pray his own agenda; he listened for God's. That was Elijah's primary mode of prayer. There is no difference between his humanity and ours. But the difference between his orientation in prayer and ours is night and day.

YOUR SOULSHIFT

Think of your prayer life as a pie graph for a moment. Give your prayer pie graph only two slices. The first slice is how much time you spend asking God for things you want. The second slice is how much time you spend listening for what God wants. Draw it out on a piece of paper and be honest with yourself. What does this graph reveal?

Can you think of something God might want that may actually hurt your selfish interests? For example, is it possible that God might want you to pray for political realities that simply are not in your own personal best interests?

DAY
2

1 KINGS 18; PROVERBS 18:1-13

In Scripture, there is a distinction between casual and faithful listening. Often, the first is translated as *listen*. The second is translated as *hear*. Deuteronomy 6:4 starts, "Hear, O Israel!" It implies more than just registering sounds on the mind. It indicates more than being able to repeat back what was said. It implies listening in a way that will lead to acting on what you hear. Ask to Listen means shifting to this second kind of listening: faithful listening.

Elijah listened this way. First, in yesterday's reading, he listened for God's will. Elijah's primary concern was to discern God's heart and mind, not to make known his own. He certainly did ask as well. But his asking was secondary. How do you make this sub-shift from disinterested listening to faithful listening? You act on what you hear. Romans 12 starts the second major section of Romans this way: "Therefore, I urge you, brothers, in view of God's mercy, to offer your bodies as living sacrifices, holy and pleasing to God." Most of the time we hear 12:1 preached separately from 12:2: "Then you will be able to test and approve what God's will is—his good, pleasing and perfect will." The connection means that if you are not ready and willing to faithfully act on what you hear, listening is futile.

If you are willing to faithfully act on what you hear, you have a promise. If you are ready and willing to do anything, say anything, go anywhere, give up anything, take up anything, suffer anything, and sacrifice anything, then (and only then) you have a promise. The promise is that you will be able to discern God's will.

Elijah was willing to take a risk. That is why his listening was productive. Fewer Christians listen than ask. Even fewer Christians listen faithfully, ready and willing to act on what they hear, no matter the cost. Elijah immediately moved from his prayer for it not to rain to confronting the wicked king Ahab who was a worshiper of Baal. He was unjust, violent, and ambitious. Elijah told Ahab it would not rain until Elijah said so. Here is what that means: On hearing God's will, Elijah acted on it in public. In acting on God's will, Elijah signed his own death warrant.

"He who answers before listening—that is his folly and his shame."
—Proverbs 18:13

The Old Testament prescribed stoning for false prophets. One drop of rain would make Elijah a false prophet and Ahab would be justified in having him slain. Further, even if he succeeded in hiding from Ahab, any Israelite could kill him if it rained. Elijah did not just listen casually; he listened faithfully. He was ready and willing to act on what he heard no matter the cost. Are you?

YOUR SOULSHIFT

What could God possibly ask of you that you would refuse to do? Make a list and then take it to God and ask him to make you willing to surrender to him.

If you can, pray this prayer, "Lord Jesus, I will go anywhere, do anything, say anything, give up anything, and take up anything if you ask it. I surrender my entire life, future, and all my dreams to you. Your will be done."

Elijah prayed God's agenda first and foremost, even when it hurt. This is at the heart of shifting from Ask to Listen. It is not that we stop asking God to do things. We change the nature of the requests. We start asking God to do his will, even when that will is against ours.

This is the number one way to increase your prayer life in quantity and quality: Take a risk. This is especially true if you risk your future, fortune, or life. It is easy to sit back telling others what they should do or should not do. It is much harder to get in the middle of the action and risk yourself for what you think is right.

In the U.S., we have insurance that minimizes risk for cars, houses, medicine, and even liability for our wrong actions. We have consumer reports to show us the safest vehicle and most risk-free gadgets. We plan our retirement at the beginning of our working years so that we are secure in the end. All of these are good things. The problem is that risk becomes a sanitized concept. Risk is something we get covered for; something we hedge; something we guard against. We do not increase our risk on purpose.

After a long time of listening for God's will in their lives, my sister-in-law and her husband moved to an inner city to copastor a church plant. They received some interesting responses to their sense of God's will for them. "Is this neighborhood safe?" Of course not. That is why they wanted to plant a church there. During a prayer walk for the church, I felt my own earnestness in prayer rise as I thought about my future nephews or nieces living here. "God protect them!" I started to pray. Then, I realized there were plenty of children already in this neighborhood not here by choice but by circumstance. "God rescue this neighborhood!" I ended. Increased risk causes increased prayer.

"Courage is fear that has said its prayers."
—Dorothy Bernard

To "call out for insight and cry aloud for understanding" (Prov. 2:3) is as natural as breathing when you are risking something deeply valuable to you. Where are your kingdom risks?

YOUR SOULSHᴵFT

What are you currently risking for God? Name specific things. Is there any part of your life that carries significant risk because you think it is God's will? Has Christ asked you to do something you are refusing because of the risk it entails? Think and pray about that for a moment. Listen. If something comes to mind, write it down. Share it with someone you trust. Listen to see if this is a risk God would have you take.

Even Elijah eventually broke down in the face of risk. It took three years and a direct threat on his life, but he did break down (1 Kings 19). What are some lessons you can learn from Elijah's breakdown in the face of risk? How can you better face those moments of fear, depression, exhaustion, and loneliness?

DAY
4

Ask Elijah about his prayer life, and you will know that God's directions change. Sometimes they do a U-turn. In one verse, Elijah was praying that it would not rain; in the next, he was praying that it would rain. Both were equally risky. Both put Elijah's reputation and security on the line. But they were opposite prayers. One day God did not want it to rain; the next day rain was on order. Both days, Elijah was in step with the Spirit of God.

Elijah discerned the reason behind the specific will of God for the moment. The rain ending was intended to show God's people their trust was in the wrong place. The rain beginning was intended to do the same. God's larger will never changes. In another way, though, God's direction does change. The only way to discern the change is to listen. Is that the way prayer is for us? Or do we pray the same prayer today that we prayed three years ago? Do we pursue the same things?

One day a single mother prays for her child's confidence to grow; two years later she prays for the child to be humbled. Two different situations, two different prayers, one reason: the desire for a Christlike character. One day a teacher prays for fewer students in his classroom because teaching reading is hard with crowded rooms; three years later he prays for more students to keep the school's finances afloat. One day a farmer prays God would help him acquire more land so he can give more; ten years later he prays God would help him find a buyer so he can give more. Asking is not ruled out of the listening life. Asking doesn't go away; it simply steps back and gets in line behind listening for God's will.

For the immature Christian, all prayers are primarily requests for blessing. For faithful Christians, listening is in the driver's seat; asking rides shotgun. Immature Christians inform God of their will; faithful Christians ask to know God's will. Immature Christians worry God may tell them no; faithful Christians worry they may say no to God. That is the difference in the shift from Ask to Listen.

> "Your own ears will hear him. Right behind you a voice will say, 'This is the way you should go,' whether to the right or to the left."
>
> —Isaiah 30:21 NLT

This shift is not a one-way arrow (our requests to God), but a circle. The circle cycles from listening to risking to asking to listening, and so on. We listen for God's will; we risk ourselves for it. We then ask Christ to do his will now that our best interests are intertwined with his. Then we return to listening again. If we forget the last step, we cement our lives in a pattern of behavior that one day will be outside of the will of God. Without thinking, we keep turning left when God turns right.

YOUR SOULSHIFT

Can you think of someone who is a good example of the listening cycle of prayer (listening, risking, asking, listening for change)?

Has there been a time when you were tempted to stay in the same direction or place, when God's will was to change directions or places?

What are some of the guiding principles you have learned for discerning direction changes from God?

PSALM 29; 1 KINGS 19:12

One day Elijah prayed and fire fell, skies opened, and a drought was lifted. So Elijah prayed, listened, and heard a response in fire, wind, and rain. The next day, he was scared, depressed, and lonely—typical ministry burnout and adrenaline drop on a massive scale. So he listened for God to get through to him. He didn't necessarily expect a voice. He looked for God to get through in the ways God had come through before.

A fire came—God had spoken that way before on Mount Carmel—this time, no voice of God. A whirlwind—God had spoken that way before—this time, no message from God. Then all was calm, quiet, and peaceful. That day, God chose to get through as a still, small voice.

The typical interpretation of this passage is that you need to be quiet if you want to hear from God. That is more often true than not, but it is not the message of this story. Elijah heard through fire, storms, wind, and even ravens. But this time, God spoke in the quiet. The real message is that you cannot predict how God will speak. God has spoken to people I know through rock songs, movies, hymns, novels, and nature. You have to be ready to receive.

Have you ever heard someone speaking and something convinced you that they were the words of God for you? Or perhaps it came in silence. Maybe you asked God a question in the stillness of your mind and the surrender of your heart, and a phrase came to mind you would have never dreamed up on your own. The point is God can and does use strange ways to get through to us. From fires, earthquakes, and rain to silence, songs, and strangers, God will get through. That is, if we are earnestly listening and looking for God to do so. Are you?

"The voice of the LORD strikes with flashes of lightening."

—Psalm 29:7

YOUR SOULSHIFT

God's voice comes to us as power and whisper, majesty and small voice. It is both truth and grace, mercy and justice. If God comes to us in such a variety of ways, how do we know when it is God?

We walk by faith not by sight as Christians. How is listening for God an act of extreme faith?

Is it right to act on something we believe we have heard from God even if we are not absolutely sure it is God's guidance we are following? Why or why not? When?

GROUP DISCUSSION GUIDE

The listening cycle was the focus of this week's reading: listen for God's will; risk yourself for his will; ask him to accomplish his will; and listen for his will to change. Listen, risk, ask, listen. During this week's discussion, be honest about the difficulty of this view of prayer.

LEADER TIPS

Since Elijah's story forms the backbone of this week's reading, be sure you are familiar with the details of the story that move from the drought and famine through to the cave. Have those passages marked in your Bible.

Try to remember a time when you were asked to risk something for God's will. Draw the emotions back to mind. What helped you be obedient? That internal reflection will prepare you with empathy.

QUESTIONS

What changes in your prayer life would this week's readings require if you were to take them seriously and apply them fully?

The readings try to unite listening with obeying and hearing with risking. What emotions emerged for you as you thought of prayer life as an active life of risk?

Were there any risks you sensed God leading you to take as you read through the readings this week? How can the group support you in those risks?

Day four's reading suggested God's directions can change even though his will is the same. Is there anything in your life that was once a direction from God that you think might be changing? What kinds of directions from God will not change for us?

Day five's reading suggested that God's way of communicating with us can change radically from time to time. Can you think of a time when God communicated in strange ways to you?

GROUP ACTIVITY

Ask God to give the group some ideas of risks they could take to participate in Christ's work in the world. Spend two to three minutes in silent listening prayer. Ask the members to write down what comes to mind. Share the lists with the group. Ask the group to pray over the list, and come back to the next meeting with the top two things they think the group can risk.

WEEK 3

A LISTENING LIFE

"To my surprise, Jesus is not content with getting me to obey him. Rather, he wants his voice to resonate with mine. He wants me to think his thoughts after him. He is calling you out of the white noise of voices you're used to into a silence that is very strange but true. In that silence, God speaks in you."[3]

DAY
1

PSALM 63:1-8; MATTHEW 4:1-4

There is a reason we call the move from Ask to Listen a shift of the soul. If listening was merely a technique for prayer, it would not need to be called a SoulShift. The shift from Ask to Listen is a move from one way of living to another. It is a way of being that goes with you into all areas of life.

Your spiritual practices can show whether you are asking or listening. You know you are asking when you engage in spiritual disciplines to accomplish or get something other than being with God. Scripture reading, fasting, praying, giving, visiting, serving, and seeking justice can all become attempts to manipulate God. Scripture reading then becomes frustrating when you don't get anything out of it. Fasting becomes frustrating when it is uncomfortable and nothing seems to get accomplished. Giving becomes burdensome because it is not getting.

"There is not in the world a kind of life more sweet and delightful, than that of a continual conversation with God; those only can comprehend it who practice and experience it."

—Brother Lawrence

That's why we look for more satisfying or exciting places than the church to give our money. Serving is draining because it is also giving, not getting.

When we learn to listen to and for God in all things, spiritual disciplines become a way of receiving the presence of Christ.

We give knowing that we receive a unique encounter with God. We serve knowing we are served by being with God. We visit knowing we will be visited by the Spirit of God. Enjoying Christ's presence in whatever way God gives it is the benefit of the Christian practices (Matt. 28:19–20).

When this shift occurs, Scripture reading becomes a way of listening. We listen more carefully and longer. We take one verse and keep listening *through* it. We do not listen for Scripture after all; we listen for God. We want to hear the Spirit of Christ. When we shift from Ask to Listen, fasting becomes an invitation more than a discipline. Christ promises to meet us there. So, we fast as a way of listening. The hunger pangs are messages from God that Christ is with the hungry. After we have made this shift, when we visit the sick, we go to listen not to speak. We no longer worry, "What should I say?" We go to listen for Christ, worship together, and find him there speaking through it.

A listening faith is not something that comes automatically or immediately. The listening life begins with attempts to attend to God's ways of getting through. Forgetfulness of God is the natural enemy. Over time, by God's grace, forgetfulness is replaced by a full sense that we truly have an Immanuel, God with us.

YOUR SOULshift

Have you ever tried to practice the presence of God for an entire day? Consider making the next twenty-four hours an experiment. See how many of those hours you can remain aware of the presence of God. In your eating, playing, working, and relating, draw your attention to God as often as possible. Do not guilt yourself when you realize your mind wandered from God. Instead thank the Spirit for bringing your mind back to God in that moment.

DAY

2

JAMES 1:2-4; 2 CORINTHIANS 4:16-18; 1 THESSALONIANS 5:16-18

Is there a more offensive statement to the suffering Christian than James' instruction to consider trials a joy? Imagine telling a friend who has suddenly lost someone close to them to "consider it pure joy." We don't say things like that if we care about people. Right?

James did say it though. Consider it pure joy. Why? Apparently the Christians to whom James was writing knew that suffering was a productive event. They knew that suffering was not a pain to be avoided, an obstacle to be overcome, or a mark on the character of God. Human suffering, to James and his scattered church, was one of the primary ways God got through to them. In suffering, patience was forged, perseverance was formed, and faith was proved.

> "Consider it pure joy, my brothers, whenever you face trials of many kinds."
>
> —James 1:2

In James' mind, suffering was not a question to put to God: "If you are a good God, how can you allow so much pain in the world?" That would be like handing a final exam back to the teacher and saying, "You answer it. Let's see how you do!" Or it might be more like throwing the test down on the ground in front of the teacher, yelling, "This isn't fair!" and stomping out of the room. Who fails the test in this scene—student or teacher?

If we think the teacher failed in this scenario, we have lost our way. The student failed for not taking the test, disrespecting the teacher, and blaming the teacher for the student's own lack of character and preparation. God is not being tested by our trials and temptations; we are.

James told us that anything that tests our faith offers a priceless opportunity for growth in Christ. Does this mean that we should be thankful for pain and suffering? No, not exactly. Instead, we are thankful for the opportunity pain and suffering bear with them. We listen through pain. Christ was a man well acquainted with suffering. He told us that we would have to pick up our cross and follow him. To become like him, we must become well acquainted with our own suffering and that of others. Rather than attempt to ignore our pain, numb it, or shortcut it, Christians recognize pain as a way of listening to God.

When pain tempts us toward mocking God, our resistance to the temptation builds the muscle of faith. When suffering weighs us down toward depression, our intentional gratitude for God's presence builds the muscle of faith. When grief burdens the soul, listening to God empowers us to mourn well and receive the comfort we need. When we learn to listen through pain, we learn that there is no life circumstance in which we cannot listen to God.

YOUR SOULSHiFT

Make a list of the pains you are facing in life currently or recently. Mention each one to God and tell him you want to hear anything the Spirit would say to you about them. Note any thoughts that come to mind as you pray.

ISAIAH 58:1-9

Do you see Christ in the suffering of the poor? Christ continually aligned himself with the poor and oppressed. Give kindness to the poor, and you have lent to the Lord (Prov. 19:17). When you

> "Do not turn your face away from any of the poor, so that God's face will not be turned away from you."
>
> —Tobit 4:7

clothe the hungry, feed the poor, and visit the imprisoned, you actually do these things for Christ. In the face of those who suffer injustice on a daily basis, we find the face of the One who came to proclaim good news to the poor.

The practice of listening to the oppressed does not come from a naïve belief that they have the answer. They may not have the answer to the world's problems, but they do have a first-hand experience of its problems. Sin is not an abstract or internal idea for them. For them, sin is real, external, and shapes their lives. The sin of greed presses down their lives to below living wages. The sin of pride scoffs at them and calls them worthless, lazy, or scum of the earth. The sin of hatred puts a boot on their neck or a machete on their wrist.

Part of the shift from Ask to Listen is learning to seek God where Christ promises to be, not where you want him to be. God promises to meet us in the poor and oppressed. The immigrant, the person without potential income, and the abandoned of the world are windows into the heart of God. The question is, are you listening through them? To hear from God in this way, you have to meet people who are oppressed without judgment in your heart, prepackaged defenses, and condescension. You have to meet them expecting that God will somehow get through to you *through* them. Exodus teaches that God hears the cry of the oppressed. Psalm 9:12 says that God does not ignore the cry of the poor. Proverbs 21:13 teaches that if we ignore the cry of the poor and oppressed, then our own prayers will not be answered. Matthew says that to love the poor is to love Christ.

Pray today, "God, send the poor and oppressed across my path, or send me to them." Watch for the answer. Then listen through them for Christ's voice.

YOUR SOULSHIFT

How could you put yourself in a place where you are more likely to be able to listen through the poor and oppressed this week?

When was the last time you listened to a person of another skin color about issues of racism and cultural oppression? Spend fifteen minutes today researching an area of injustice in order to understand more.

DAY
4

MATTHEW 25:31-46; JAMES 5:13-15

The sick used to be confined to their own beds with doctors making house calls. Now the critically ill suffer in buildings dedicated to sickness and dying. We now have new diseases bred by these buildings of healing. The people in most critical need are isolated from the outside world. The elderly and dying are given their own communities. Our entire society seeks to insulate itself from the sick, to avoid seeing the dying, and to dress up the dead as if they were living once they have passed. These things are not evil; they simply make it easier for us to avoid doing one simple command: visit the sick.

> "I have an opportunity to be with Jesus twenty-four hours a day."
> —Mother Teresa

Pastors need to visit the sick, of course, like every other Christian. They visit the sick because they are Christians not because they are pastors. Why should we all do this? Christ promises to be present with the sick. And Christ promises that what we do for the sick, we actually do for him. When we visit the sick, we visit Jesus Christ. Every time you hear that someone is seriously ill, you have just received an invitation from Christ. The sick are living invitations to be with Christ.

"I am too busy," you may say. Do you have time for TV, the newspaper, or social media? Don't be too busy for Christ while you make time for distractions. "They may not want me to come." You are not going for them, but for you and for Christ. They may even ask you to leave. Christ was rejected by those he came to save. "It drains me emotionally." Even Christ felt power go out from him. Do you avoid work because it drains you? Do you avoid your spouse when he or she has an emotional burden for you to bear? "I wouldn't know what to say." Say that you do not know what to say. After all, you are not going for the purpose of saying something. You are going to listen. This is a shift from Ask to Listen. Go and listen. Ask them their favorite Scriptures or hymns, and then listen. Ask what is on their minds and listen. Or go and see what they say. Just show up. Follow their lead on what they want to talk about. Be willing to sit in silence, which is a form of listening.

It has often been said that 90 percent of ministry is showing up. It is amazing what God can do when we just show up. Showing up is the hard part, but make the effort to go and visit the sick. And when you do, go to listen. Do not assume you need to fix anything or ease any pain. Go, listen, and wait. Christ will get through to you there.

YOUR SOULSHIFT

Can you think of a time God has gotten through to you via someone who was sick? What did you specifically learn from that encounter?

What are the kinds of things we can be reminded of through regular contact with those who are sick?

Consider shut-ins, nursing home residents, and relationships connected to your group. Which sick person could you visit this week? Why not go?

DAY
5

HEBREWS 13:3; MATTHEW 25:31-46

One day, I went to volunteer at a local prison. After I shared the short version of my story with sin, depression, suicide attempts, and then salvation, another man about my age raised his hand. He was wearing the khaki-colored uniform just like the rest of the room. His badge read "Offender" in bright red capital letters. It was his label. He said, "I wonder if economic class has anything to do with this. I think the expectations of your social class for your success caused your failures to be more difficult for you than they would be for me. None of the things you mentioned would cause me depression; everyone I knew was doing them." Is this how you expect a prisoner to speak? It was not what I expected.

>❦
>
> "He has sent me to proclaim freedom for the prisoners."
>
> —Luke 4:18

I had prayed before going into the prison that day that God would help me listen through the prisoners to catch glimpses of Christ. I stumbled over my words for a moment while I tried to listen for Christ. As I listened, I realized this prisoner may be right. He had probably fallen as short of his family's and friends' expectations as I had mine. He was simply surrounded by lower expectations. I could no longer look at this person as an "Offender" who was different than me. I saw him as if he was me. Had I been with his family, neighborhood, school, and friends, I might be in prison by force, not by choice. God got through to me using that prisoner.

"People just are not knocking down the doors to get involved in prison ministry," a former prison chaplain, now prison volunteer, said to me. Participating in prison ministry can be challenging, but Christ said he will be there. He promised to reward Christians who visited those in prison. If the church remembered these truths and believed them, prison doors might be knocked down. We have forgotten.

Sometime over the next year, go to prison. Look into the eyes of someone who will never again see the outside world. Meet people studying for Christian ministry in prison. Learn the life stories of those who live behind bars. Or at least, visit a local jail where most have a short-term stay. Learn the power of one voice, act of love, word of grace, intervention, or way out. It will change your life and possibly have an impact beyond what you imagine.

YOUR SOULSHIFT

Do you personally know anyone who is currently in prison? How might you increase your contact with them so that you can hear from Christ through them?

Take a few minutes to listen to what the Spirit might say to you about visiting prison. Surrender yourself to the possibility that God might ask you to go. Once you are willing, listen for what God brings to mind. Write it down and share it with someone else.

GROUP DISCUSSION GUIDE

This week may have caught you by surprise. You thought this was about prayer. Isn't prayer something we do in private? Works of mercy or social justice are different than learning to listen to God in prayer. Right? Wrong. You cannot listen clearly to God unless you are involved in the lives of the poor, oppressed, sick, or imprisoned. Your defenses will be too high, justifications too strong, and judgment of others will speak too loudly. Not every Christian does all of these things, but all faithful Christians do some of these. If you have never listened to "the least of these," you have been ignoring the voice of God.

LEADER TIPS

This week is a week about active listening. Try to avoid any division between listening for and serving God.

It may be difficult for you to lead this week's discussion if you have no experience with the poor, oppressed, sick, or imprisoned. Consider finding a way to go to a nursing home, mission, or prison before the group meeting to become more familiar.

Remember that these activities do not make you more righteous. Instead, they are places where you can meet Christ. Christ—not our good deeds—makes us holy. This is a key distinction.

QUESTIONS

In most discussions of faith, our works of compassion and devotion are two separate things. We pray as an act of devotion; we give as an act of compassion. How are compassion and devotion increased when we keep them together?

How can visiting the sick or imprisoned and listening to the poor or oppressed help us hear God better?

What is the difference between listening *to* the poor, sick, and imprisoned and listening for God *through* the poor, sick, and imprisoned?

What was one of the most helpful parts of the reading for you this week? What did it specifically help you do?

What do the readings regarding risky prayers and the listening life have in common?

There is a common thread between our suffering and that of others: both are key places where God speaks. Do you have experiences that show this is the case?

ACTIVITY

Decide as a group on a particular category of persons from the sheep and goats passage (Matt. 25:31–46) that your group can minister to and listen for God through. Make a specific goal-oriented plan that will put you in face-to-face ministry with that group within a month.

WEEK 4

LISTENING FOR GOD'S WILL

"This is how it is with God. There he sits with us, longing
to communicate. He would celebrate us and inspire us
if only we would disconnect with the other voices in
our lives to hear his voice."[4]

DAY
1

2 CHRONICLES 1:7-12; PROVERBS 2:1-22; JAMES 1:5-8

What situation, crisis, problem, or issue is screaming out for insight? What decision calls out for discernment? For what would you be willing to beg for wisdom? Right now, pause, think, listen, and write what comes to mind in the margin.

Now take note of what James promises in verse 5: Ask and God will give wisdom. God gives wisdom "generously to all without finding fault" (James 1:5). So that means your lack of flawless living does not affect God's willingness to give wisdom. That's good news! God wants to "talk" in the sense of getting through to you. He wants to help you "learn to know [his] will for you, which is good and pleasing and perfect" (Rom. 12:2 NLT). These things are central to the heart of God. The Father promises that if you seek him with all your heart, you will find him. He wants, promises, and is determined to get through to you, if you are willing to listen.

Take a few minutes in silence to center your attention on God. Bring your concern, issue, or question to mind. It should be something for which you would like to receive wisdom. Then wrestle with yourself internally until you can with absolute, unflinching honesty tell God you are willing to do whatever he might ask you to do or believe whatever he might ask you to believe. Next, say these words out loud to God: "Lord, you have promised to give wisdom to those who ask. I pray that you would fulfill your promise to me. I believe you will. Whatever you bring to mind next, I am going to write down in case it is from you. Please do not let me be deceived." Whisper if you have to, but still say it. Finally, listen. There will likely not be an audible voice. Turn your attention inward to the Spirit. Write down any phrases, images, or memories that come to mind.

> "If any of you lacks wisdom, he should ask God, who gives generously to all without finding fault, and it will be given to him."
>
> —James 1:5

YOUR SOULSHIFT

Write down three situations for which you need insight, discernment, or wisdom.

Sometime today find a place where you can talk to God out loud about these three things. Turn off the radio during your commute, go into an empty closet, take a walk in the woods, or whisper your thoughts to God behind a closed door. Tell God you trust him to guide you. Write down any insights that come during that prayer time. Also, keep your spiritual antennae up the rest of the day for God to get through in strange and unique ways. If you ask, God will give wisdom.

DAY
2

ROMANS 12:1-3; 1 CORINTHIANS 10:23-24

Sarah was faced with deciding between becoming a writer or nurse. Tim needed to decide whether to move his family for a new job that fit his skills and passions or stay where he was to provide stability for his children. Does God have a will on these matters? How could they know?

God gives wisdom to those who seek it and trust that they will receive it. Wisdom is not a golden tablet descending from the sky, however. And it doesn't usually come in a flash of blinding light. Instead a wise person "gives thought to his ways" (Prov. 21:29), does not make hasty decisions, only acts with full knowledge (Prov. 19:2), and balances one person's counsel against another (Prov. 18:17). Romans 12 reminds us that surrendering our lives is necessary to discerning God's will. All of this teaches us to:

- Get all the necessary information;
- Take time, without procrastinating, to make a good choice;
- Get more than one wise and mature Christian's opinion;
- Honestly and fully surrender your own selfish desires (including any sins); and
- Try to discern God's desires.

Think about a significant decision you have to make. Have you done these things? Sarah had all the knowledge and counsel she needed about writing and nursing. What she did not have was a willing heart. She made it clear to God that she would not leave the country. Later, she was called to medical missions work. Only when Sarah surrendered did she discern God's will. Tim had a willing heart and pure motives. He wanted what was righteous from God's perspective. What he did not have was all the information. He knew a promotion would mean better pay, better benefits, and less college debt for his kids. What he had not learned was that a move would take them to a town without a healthy and vital church community to which he could trust his children's spiritual formation. Once he visited the town, Tim gathered this information. Then his willing heart knew what to do.

"Therefore, I urge you, brothers, in view of God's mercy, to offer your bodies as living sacrifices, holy and pleasing to God . . . Then you will be able to test and approve what God's will is—his good, pleasing and perfect will."

—Romans 12:1–2

YOUR SOULSHIFT

Think of a life decision you are facing. From the list above, what area are you lacking? Focus on that weakest area all day. Send the e-mails, make the phone calls, do the searches, and ask the questions. Or if surrender is the issue, take time to journal. Get on your knees in prayer. Beg God to make you willing. Imagine what Christ might ask, and tell him out loud, "Your will be done" until you can mean it.

DAY
3

MALACHI 4:1-6; ISAIAH 61:1-7

My wife, Holly, and I learned that for ten years, Tara had coped with the stress of life, family, past abuse, and ministry by abusing alcohol and prescription drugs. The result was ten years of bondage and numbness to her husband, shame in worship services, and fear of being discovered in the small town where she was an actively involved Christian.

Tara, Holly, and I prayed. I gave her questions to ask God, and she told me what came to mind when she asked. Some people see images; others retrieve memories or have complete thoughts like a conversation. Tara had a conversation about generational sins, emotional bondage, grace, and God's power to deliver.

Tara told God that she would trust in his deliverance. She went to the car, her suitcase, and her purse to retrieve all of the alcohol and pills. She felt that God had asked her to get rid of them. With shaking hands, trembling body, and flowing tears, she flushed her addiction away.

Over the next few months, we prayed together several times over the phone. She obeyed whatever she sensed God saying. God led her to take her first scary step toward confession in a small town, join a support group, and find a counselor. Every few months she sends us an e-mail, celebrating another milestone of sobriety.

Christ does not want to get through to us for the sake of being heard; he wants to bring deep healing. If God can resurrect Jesus from the dead, he can resurrect your life from its bondage. God always wants to break the power of sin. It may not be immediate and it may take years of listening, trusting, obeying, and confessing. Yet I believe part of the journey from Ask to Listen is listening for God's prescriptions for healing. These are part of his will for you.

"The LORD hears his people when they call to him for help. He rescues them from all their troubles."

—Psalm 34:17 NLT

YOUR SOULSHIFT

Spend time today listening to God about healing. Are there areas in your life whether emotional, physical, or spiritual where you are wounded? Are there particular sins that hold you captive? Call these needs for healing and God's presence to mind. Then simply listen. If you think best in journaling, consider writing down things that come to mind.

Pray together with a close friend regarding a deep wound in your life. Let him or her tell you the questions to ask God. They can be simple questions such as, "What do you want to say to me today, Lord?" or, "Can you please help me forgive?" Share with your friend what you see, hear, or think. Then let him or her guide you in asking more questions.

DAY
4

ECCLESIASTES 3:1-2; JOB 38

The key difference when we shift from Ask to Listen is that we start asking different sorts of questions once we see that God's questions are larger than ours. We ask God what questions to ask.

Tessa wanted to know what God's will was for her career. She did not feel called in a particular direction, and she didn't want to make a wrong decision. She brought that question to God. Over time she realized God's Spirit was asking a very different set of questions. Tessa wanted to know what career would best fit her gifts so she could be successful and feel fulfilled at the same time. God started to show her how self-centered this way of questioning was. God started giving her questions to ask instead.

Here are some of them she discerned over time: Who are you trying to impress with your success and giftedness? What does a good life look like? Why is the gap between the rich and poor countries larger now than ever? Why are we one of the most advanced societies in the world, yet still unaware of the needs of orphans? Why does the worst crime happen in the worst neighborhoods? What makes those neighborhoods bad in the first place? Why are mainline churches shrinking while still trying to do good? Why are so many evangelicals angry and judgmental, while they proclaim a gospel of good news and grace?

These questions led Tessa down a very different road than she thought she would travel. She was not called to pastoral ministry. Yet she couldn't face the selfishness in her heart, the evil in the world, or the divisions in the church without doing something. Before she started praying, Tessa thought she would study law.

After significant time listening, she *knew* she would study law. The difference? Her aim was radically different. Success was not necessarily a big firm partnership or a high court position, but using law to protect the poor, helping churches share faith and do good at the same time, and participating in answering God's questions. Success required seeing the big picture of the evil in the world and seeking big-picture solutions. Tessa's questions brought her to listen and follow the Spirit. God's questions welcome our own.

> "I had a thousand questions to ask God; but when I met him they all fled and didn't seem to matter."
>
> —Christopher Morley

YOUR SOULSHIFT

What are the most pressing questions for you lately? List them and take a few minutes to bring these questions to God. Ask God to show you the questions he would ask in response. If any come to mind, write them down.

What do God's questions teach you?

DAY
5

MATTHEW 4:1-11; ISAIAH 30:1-21

In Matthew 4, Jesus was led into the wilderness by the Spirit. The Spirit did not tempt Jesus, but led him into a place where temptation would be strong. Jesus was tested, strengthened, and confirmed through that test, part of which was that the kingdoms of the world were spread at his feet. Faithful followers of Christ are tested in similar ways. We are tempted to take shortcuts and obtain provision that God isn't offering (turn stones to bread), expect him to protect us from our own consequences (jump from the pinnacle of the temple), and receive his promises without the required process (worship false gods in exchange for the kingdoms of the world). These are temptations to shortcut the will of God. They are the asking life: give me pleasure, protection, and power.

You don't need to go the long way; you can have it today. All you need to do is worship the corporation, money, or power; worship a relational network, career, idea, or way of life; bend your knee, and all you hoped to receive in the end will be yours in the beginning. Ask to receive that, and you may hear a voice responding, "Yes." But it won't be God's voice.

Do not pester God for your success, comfort, wealth, health, beauty, and fame. These things are always empty in the end. They are momentary, fragile, and do not give the happiness they promise.

> *"There are two kinds of people in the end: those who say to God, 'Thy will be done,' and those to whom God says, in the end, 'Thy will be done.'"*
>
> —C. S. Lewis

Instead, beg God to guide you in his will. Christ's rule and reign should be your desire, not your own rule and reign. God's desires and hopes should be your dream, not your own fantasies of a perfect life. Listen for the ancient way of God. Then you will hear a voice saying, "This is the way; walk in it" (Isa. 30:21).

YOUR SOULSHⁱFT

There are plenty of preachers who will tell you to "name it and claim it" so that you can have the best possible life now. After reading from Matthew and Isaiah, write a paraphrase message from God to those preachers.

How do you know the difference between a shortcut offered as temptation and the reward given by God for faithfulness and patience?

What lingering questions do you have about the shift from Ask to Listen as a way of life? Where in Scripture might you find some answers or at least some questions that are larger than yours?

GROUP DISCUSSION GUIDE

Congratulations! You have made it through this Bible study for the SoulShift from Ask to Listen. You will keep benefiting from these concepts only if you put them into practice. Spend this week's session attempting to structure into your group and individual lives patterns of listening prayer.

LEADER TIPS

This session should cover the key components of this week's readings on discerning God's will, as well as wrap up your study of shifting from Ask to Listen.

Sometimes the question of discerning God's will brings up anxious situations for people in your group. Be prepared to shepherd the group in caring for individuals whose lives are in flux or uncertainty. You will want to balance care with boundaries so that each member has time to hear and be heard.

Spend some time listening to God before your group meets. Quiet yourself. Bring your concerns or confusions to him. Listen for his questions and concerns. Let that time adjust this guide in any way necessary.

QUESTIONS

Was there a time in your life when you clearly felt God's guidance, acted on it in faith, and the situation seemed to eventually demonstrate God's involvement in your life?

Is there a situation or uncertainty in your life right now for which you feel the need to discern God's will?

Is there an area of your life where you think God's will requires a change in direction?

How has the way you think about and practiced prayer changed over the past month?

What are some specific listening practices your group can turn into habits?

"Once you hear from God, 'Yes' is the only reply. We want to hear from him. That's for sure. But are we ready to say yes? Are we ready to listen and do whatever he asks?"[5]

NOTES

1. Steve DeNeff and David Drury, *SoulShift: The Measure of a Life Transformed* (Indianapolis, Ind.: Wesleyan Publishing House, 2011), 100.

2. Ibid., 96.

3. Ibid., 93.

4. Ibid., 99.

5. Ibid., 104.